the guide to owning a Bulldog

Eve Adamson

T.F.H. Publications, Inc.
One TFH Plaza
Third and Union Avenues
Neptune City, NJ 07753

Library of Congress Cataloging-in-Publication Data
Adamson, Eve.
The guide to owning a bulldog / Eve Adamson.
p. cm.
ISBN 0-7938-1900-8 (alk. paper)
1. Bulldog. I. Title.
SF429.B85A33 2004
636.72--dc22
2004000005

t.f.h.

www.tfh.com

Contents

Given the proper care and lots of love, your Bulldog will be your friend for life.

The History of the Bulldog

The handsome, burly Bulldog makes a placid and agreeable friend to humankind. Known for his characteristically massive head, pendulous jowls, wrinkled brow, and muscle-bound shoulders, the Bulldog can scarcely be mistaken for any other breed. Often used as a logo or mascot for everything from beer to sports teams to the United States Marine Corps, Bulldogs are among the most recognized of breeds, especially in England, where the Bulldog is the national breed and a symbol of indomitable British spirit.

However, the Bulldog breed hardly came about naturally. A "created" breed designed to fight bulls for sport, the Bulldog is a direct product of purposeful breeding, and every unique physical characteristic of the Bulldog had a specific function. When the cruel sport of bullbaiting became illegal, the Bulldog didn't die with it. Instead, he evolved with the times and according to the desires of those breeders determined to keep him.

The Bulldog has an easygoing disposition and is the perfect pet for limited quarters.

How did the Bulldog evolve from a game and fearsome fighter to a friendly family companion in so short a time? The story begins in England.

FROM BUTCHER'S HELPER TO BULLBAITER

Centuries ago, strong, heavy Mastiff-type dogs worked beside butchers to guard and drive livestock, pull carts, chase vermin, and assist in hunting. These dogs had to be large and intimidating enough to control a herd of cattle, fierce enough to guard both stock and property effectively, and versatile enough to perform other duties as they arose. They had a natural tendency to bait bulls in order to keep them in line, and some individuals were, we can guess, more likely to taunt and even attack the bulls, which were dangerous and difficult to control.

From this photo it is easy to see why the Bulldog is affectionately called the "sourmug."

Throughout history, people have tended to be attracted to a good fight, whether on the playground or the battlefield, and the sight of a group of muscular dogs fighting with a massive bull was bound to attract the attention, admiration, and entrepreneurial spirit of many. One story goes that a lord spotted a group of dogs taunting a bull and asked that the event be organized for his continued pleasure and amusement.

Bearbaiting and bullbaiting (and, in fact, the baiting of any large, fierce animal) were certainly popular in Great Britain as early as the 14th or 15th century, and because bulls were easier to come by than bears, bullbaiting became the blood sport of choice for noblemen and commoners alike. Anyone could participate. A bull was tied to a stake or iron ring in the ground in an open field or other informal arena, and the dogs were let loose to attack. Sometimes the dogs latched onto a nose, their heavy jowls enclosing the bull's mouth, and the bull eventually suffocated, while other times the dogs worked the bull to exhaustion. Of course, the dogs were often tossed aside or gored by the bull's horns, and many dogs were injured and killed in a sport that was cruel to both dog and bull.

Unfortunately, the sport persisted for centuries, in part probably due to the circulation of the false notion that the practice tenderized bull meat before slaughter (no doubt the idea of some enterprising Bulldog breeder or enthusiastic gambler). The sport became a tradition, and in some areas, the principle form of entertainment. Butchers were sometimes required to subject their bulls to bullbaiting before a slaughter or else pay a fine.

Soon, Bulldogs (also sometimes called Bondogges, Boldogges, and Bandogges at the time) were bred specifically for the more lucrative job of bullbaiting, their original work as butcher's assistant long forgotten or a secondary occupation at best. The dogs used in the sport were probably taller and larger than the Bulldog we know today, but breeders looking to design the perfect bullbaiting dog encouraged the proliferation of certain key traits that still characterize Bulldogs.

The Bulldog's strong, locking jaw and underbite allowed him to latch onto the bull's nose or ear from below and hold on without being flung off. The shoulders, set so wide and to the side, allowed the Bulldog to crouch low to avoid the bull's sharp, swiping horns. The dog's sturdy, heavy bone made the dog more resilient when successfully thrown off. Finally, the Bulldog had to be so devoted that he would attack a bull when asked and persevere to the finish, to win or die for the sake of his master.

THE RISE AND FALL OF BULLBAITING

Nobody knows for sure exactly how the sport of bullbaiting began. Humans have long used animals for sport, and bullbaiting was one of the most violent examples of this human tendency. Eventually, despite the lack of animal cruelty laws, some people were bound to protest. Protest they did, and by the end of the 17th century, the sport had begun to decline in popularity and practice. In 1802, a bill to ban bullbaiting was struck down in the House of Commons, but in 1835, Parliament enacted a law banning bullbaiting, bearbaiting, dog fighting, or any other animal blood sport; it also forbade the keeping of a place, pit, or arena for such sports.

Your Bulldog will be so happy when you treat him right. He may even give you a smile.

What, then, happened to the Bulldog? In addition to the breed's fearsome nature and great courage,

Bulldogs were also so devoted to humans that many people had, in turn, become equally devoted to Bulldogs. The first Bulldoggers (as Bulldog fanciers like to call themselves), determined to preserve the breed now left without a job, quickly recognized that certain traits in the Bulldog could be a detriment. Bulldog breeding was reorganized to maintain the Bulldog's unique appearance while softening the temperament to further emphasize the breed's natural devotion and agreeable nature.

As the Bulldog continued to evolve in England and America, the breed became shorter and heavier, with a shorter muzzle, and more docile. As dog shows gained in popularity in England, Bulldogs become more popular again. In 1864, Bulldog breeders drafted a breed standard, which is a description of how the ideal specimen of a breed should look, to be used by dog show judges in evaluating different breeds. In 1875, this "Standard of Perfection" for Bulldogs was published in England.

THE BULLDOG IN AMERICA

Meanwhile, Americans began to fancy the Bulldog and show these dogs in conformation shows. The Bulldog Club of America (BCA) formed in 1890 and adopted the English breed standard. In 1896, the BCA penned its own revised standard, which has been occasionally adapted over the years, so that the description of the ideal Bulldog in America is slightly different than the description of the ideal Bulldog in England.

The Bulldog served as the basis for many other breeds, which subsequently arose through isolated regional breeding and crosses with other breeds (such as terriers). While not everyone agrees that the Bulldog is the progenitor of the American Bulldog, American Pit Bull Terrier, Staffordshire Bull Terrier, American Staffordshire Terrier, and Bullmastiff, this belief is widely accepted. The Bulldog himself has also certainly evolved in conformation since his original fighting days to become somewhat less athletic and far less aggressive. However, he has remained strong, courageous, and loyal.

Today, the BCA remains an active national breed club and the parent club of many regional Bulldog breed clubs. Officially recognized by the American Kennel Club (AKC), the BCA consists of breeders, judges, handlers, and other fanciers who agree to breed according to certain ethical principles focused around the well-being and best interests of Bulldogs, and in accordance with the official breed standard. The BCA also works to educate the public about Bulldog breeders, Bulldog care, Bulldog training, and Bulldog health. Check out their informative website at www.thebca.org.

The Characteristics of the Bulldog

Bulldogs today have the important role of human companion. While the Bulldog retains many of the characteristics that once made him a skilled and tenacious fighter, his character has mellowed through successive generations of breeding for sound and stable temperament. The Bulldog now makes an excellent house pet, mellow friend, and trustworthy confidante.

The Bulldog's stable, relaxed nature helps him to enjoy many activities, whether he is exhibiting his characteristic loose-jointed shuffling but vigorous trot around the show ring or around the block, whether he is doing lap duty during television time, or sunning himself on the floor.

The Bulldog gives the impression that he approaches life with kindness, courage, and a peaceful, stout, and solid sort of dignity. He makes a delightful family member and takes his job seriously, with just a glint of humor apparent in that wrinkled brow and those wide-set, dark eyes. Let's take a closer look at some of the other essential traits that characterize a Bulldog.

The general appearance and attitude of the Bulldog should suggest great stability, vigor, and strength.

BULLY PERSONALITY AND SPECIAL NEEDS

The Bulldog may present a scowling mug to the world, but anyone who gets to know one soon discovers how contrary his appearance is to his friendly and outgoing personality. Bulldogs are typically mellow, easy-going, and happy dogs that like nothing more than to be cuddled, rocked, kissed, adored, and pampered. For this reason, Bulldogs make excellent family pets. They don't mind child's play and can be quite good sports about being dressed up and carted around. Bulldogs adore attention, and doting children make excellent buddies for them. However, the Bulldog is not the best choice for extremely active families. No longer a breed capable of bringing down a bull, Bulldogs are not able to take on a 5-mile (or even a 1-mile) jog, and families looking for a high-energy, athletic canine companion will probably be disappointed in the Bulldog.

Even vigorous play sessions outside in the heat of summer aren't good for a Bulldog, whose short muzzle makes him susceptible to heatstroke. Bulldogs need to keep cool, stay in the air conditioning, and drink lots of water as temperatures soar. A Bulldog can still take a short walk or play outside for short periods in hot weather, but overheating is a real danger, so

Bulldogs absolutely must live inside with their people. They are vulnerable to temperature extremes and are serious about their job as human companions.

A Bulldog puppy is an adorable mass of wrinkles. Soft, loose skin is a distinct feature of the breed.

If you're not sure if you want a dog, don't look at the Bulldog. You'll fall instantly in love and want one for your own.

exercise caution during summer and in hot climates.

The Bulldog's short face, many skin wrinkles, typically sensitive skin, and large head can also potentially result in a number of health problems, from minor skin infections and eye problems to respiratory problems. Most Bullies have a reputation for being snorers, and a Bulldog snore isn't easy to ignore (although many long-time Bulldoggers swear they get used to it). Their large heads and small hips also mean that most female Bulldogs will require cesarean sections to deliver puppies, an almost certain expense that budding Bulldog breeders must consider. Unfortunately, Bulldogs also have a relatively short life span of approximately eight years.

Bulldogs absolutely must live in the house with their people because of their vulnerability to temperature extremes and because they are so serious about their job as human companions. Bulldogs are not built, physically or mentally, for solitary living. They need comfort, care, and affection as much as they need food and water.

While Bulldogs have a reputation for being placid, some make good watchdogs and will, to the shock and surprise of all who know them, quite suddenly defend a human in danger with appropriate ferocity. Don't count on a Bulldog to be a protection dog or even a watchdog, however. For the most part, they don't retain this instinct. Instead, they are sweet, lovable, and just "ugly" enough to be completely adorable.

The Standard for the Bulldog

The Bulldog breed standard is a written description of Bulldog perfection. The Bulldog Club of America (BCA), the national breed club recognized as the official parent club for Bulldogs by the American Kennel Club, originally based the Bulldog standard on the English standard.

All that this really means is that Bulldog breeders and dog show judges have a written guide with which to judge and breed Bulldogs, with the goal of continuing to improve the Bulldog, edging the breed ever closer to the official idea of perfection. Some Bulldogs may differ from the standard, and that doesn't make them any less lovable. Nevertheless, here is the official Bulldog breed standard, as approved by the American Kennel Club followed by the British breed standard approved by England's Kennel Club.

Breed standards vary from country to country and registry to registry. Always check with your breed club for the most current standard.

THE AKC STANDARD FOR THE BULLDOG

General Appearance—The perfect Bulldog must be of medium size and smooth coat; with heavy, thick-set, low-swung body, massive short-faced head, wide shoulders and sturdy limbs. The general appearance and attitude should suggest great stability, vigor and strength. The disposition should be equable and kind, resolute and courageous (not vicious or aggressive), and demeanor should be pacific and dignified. These attributes should be countenanced by the expression and behavior.

Size, Proportion, Symmetry—*Size*—The size for mature dogs is about 50 pounds; for mature bitches about 40 pounds. *Proportion*—The circumference of the skull in front of the ears should measure at least the height of the dog at the shoulders.

Bulldog pups should appear as adult Bulldogs in miniature.

Symmetry—The "points" should be well distributed and bear good relation one to the other, no feature being in such prominence from either excess or lack of quality that the animal appears deformed or ill-proportioned. *Influence of Sex*—In comparison of specimens of different sex, due allowance should be made in favor of the bitches, which do not bear the characteristics of the breed to the same degree of perfection and grandeur as do the dogs.

Head—*Eyes and Eyelids*—The eyes, seen from the front, should be situated low down in the skull, as far from the ears as possible, and their corners should be in a straight line at right angles with the stop. They should be quite in front of the head, as wide apart as possible, provided their outer corners are within the outline of the cheeks when viewed from the front. They should be quite round in form, of moderate size, neither sunken nor bulging, and in color should be very dark. The lids should cover the white of the eyeball, when the dog is looking directly forward, and the lid should show no "haw." *Ears*—The ears should be set high in the head, the front inner edge of each ear joining the outline of the skull at the top back corner of skull, so as to place them as wide apart, and as high, and as far from the eyes as possible. In size they should be small and thin. The shape termed "rose ear" is the most desirable. The

A Bulldog's ears should be small, thin, and set high on the head. They should never be cropped or carried erectly.

rose ear folds inward at its back lower edge, the upper front edge curving over, outward and backward, showing part of the inside of the burr. (The ears should not be carried erect or prick-eared or buttoned and should never be cropped.) *Skull*—The skull should be very large, and in circumference, in front of the ears, should measure at least the height of the dog at the shoulders. Viewed from the front, it should appear very high from the corner of the lower jaw to the apex of the skull, and also very broad and square. Viewed at the side, the head should appear very high, and very short from the point of the nose to occiput. The forehead should be flat (not rounded or domed), neither too prominent nor overhanging the face. *Cheeks*—The cheeks should be well rounded, protruding sideways and outward beyond the eyes. *Stop*—The temples or frontal bones should be very well defined, broad, square and high, causing a hollow or groove between the eyes. This indentation, or stop, should be both broad and deep and extend up the middle of the forehead, dividing the head vertically, being traceable to the top of the skull. *Face and Muzzle*—The face, measured from the front of the cheekbone to the tip of the nose, should be extremely short, the muzzle being very short, broad, turned upward and very deep from the corner of the eye to the corner of the mouth. *Nose*—The nose should be large, broad and black, its tip set back deeply between the eyes. The distance from bottom of stop, between the eyes, to the tip of nose should be as short as possible and not exceed the length from the tip of nose to the edge of underlip. The nostrils should be wide, large and black, with a well-defined line between them. Any nose other than black is objectionable and a brown or liver-colored nose shall ***disqualify***. *Lips*—The chops or "flews" should be thick, broad, pendant and very deep, completely overhanging the lower jaw at each side. They join the underlip in front and almost or quite cover the teeth, which should be scarcely noticeable when the mouth is closed. *Bite—Jaws*—The jaws should be massive, very broad, square and "undershot," the lower jaw projecting considerably in front of the upper jaw and turning up. *Teeth*—The teeth should be large and strong, with the canine teeth or tusks wide apart, and the six small teeth in front, between the canines, in an even, level row.

Neck, Topline, Body—*Neck*—The neck should be short, very thick, deep and strong and well arched at the back. *Topline*—There should be a slight fall in the back, close behind the shoulders (its lowest part), whence the spine should rise to the loins (the top of which should be higher than the top of the shoulders), thence curving again more suddenly to the tail, forming an arch (a very distinctive feature of the breed), termed "roach back" or, more correctly, "wheel-back." *Body*—The brisket and body should be very capacious, with full sides, well-rounded ribs and very deep from the shoulders down to its lowest part, where it joins the chest. It should be well let down between the shoulders and forelegs, giving the dog a broad, low, short-legged appearance. *Chest*—The chest should be very broad, deep and full. *Underline*—The body should be well ribbed up behind with the belly tucked up and not rotund. *Back and Loin*—The back should be short and strong, very broad at the shoulders and comparatively narrow at the loins. *Tail*—The tail may be either straight or "screwed" (but never curved or curly), and in any case must be short, hung low, with decided downward carriage, thick root and fine tip. If straight, the tail should be cylindrical and of uniform taper. If "screwed," the bends or kinks should be well defined, and they may be abrupt and even knotty, but no portion of the member should be elevated above the base or root.

Forequarters—*Shoulders*—The shoulders should be muscular, very heavy, widespread and slanting outward, giving stability and great power. *Forelegs*—The forelegs should be short, very stout, straight and muscu-

As the youngsters mature, the wrinkles and dewlaps will become more pronounced. Additionally, the muzzle and nose leather will darken.

lar, set wide apart, with well developed calves, presenting a bowed outline, but the bones of the legs should not be curved or bandy, nor the feet brought too close together. *Elbows*—The elbows should be low and stand well out and loose from the body. *Feet*—The feet should be moderate in size, compact and firmly set. Toes compact, well split up, with high knuckles and very short stubby nails. The front feet may be straight or slightly out-turned.

Hindquarters—*Legs*—The hind legs should be strong and muscular and longer than the forelegs, so as to elevate the loins above the shoulders. Hocks should be slightly bent and well let down, so as to give length and strength from the loins to hock. The lower leg should be short, straight and strong, with the stifles turned slightly outward and away from the body. The hocks are thereby made to approach each other, and the hind feet to turn outward. *Feet*—The feet should be moderate in size, compact and firmly set. Toes compact, well split up, with high knuckles and short stubby nails. The hind feet should be pointed well outward.

Coat and Skin—*Coat*—The coat should be straight, short, flat, close, of fine texture, smooth and glossy. (No fringe, feather or curl.) *Skin*—The skin should be soft and loose, especially at the head, neck and shoulders. *Wrinkles and Dewlap*—The head and face should be covered with heavy wrinkles, and at the throat, from jaw to chest, there should be two loose pendulous folds, forming the dewlap.

Color of Coat—The color of coat should be uniform, pure of its kind and brilliant. The various colors found in the breed are to be preferred in the following order: (1) red brindle, (2) all other brindles, (3) solid white, (4) solid red, fawn or fallow, (5) piebald, (6) inferior qualities of all the foregoing. *Note:* A perfect piebald is preferable to a muddy brindle or defective solid color. Solid black is very undesirable, but not so objectionable if occurring to a moderate degree in piebald patches. The brindles to be perfect should have a fine, even and equal distribution of the composite colors. In brindles and solid colors a small white patch on the chest is not considered detrimental. In piebalds the color patches should be well defined, of pure color and symmetrically distributed.

Gait—The style and carriage are peculiar, his gait being a loose-jointed, shuffling, sidewise motion, giving the characteristic "roll." The action must, however, be unrestrained, free and vigorous.

Temperament—The disposition should be equable and kind, resolute and courageous (not vicious or aggressive), and demeanor should be pacific and dignified. These attributes should be countenanced by the expression and behavior.

Scale of Points

General Properties		
Proportion and Symmetry	5	
Attitude	3	
Expression	2	
Gait	3	
Size	3	
Coat	2	
Color of Coat	4	22
Head		
Skull	5	
Cheeks	2	
Stop	4	
Eyes and Eyelids	3	
Ears	5	
Wrinkle	5	
Nose	6	
Chops	2	
Jaws	5	
Teeth	2	39
Body, Legs, etc.		
Neck	3	
Dewlap	2	
Shoulders	5	
Chest	3	
Ribs	3	
Brisket	2	
Belly	2	
Back	5	
Forelegs and Elbows	4	
Hind Legs	3	
Feet	3	
Tail	4	39
Total		100

DISQUALIFICATION

Brown or liver-colored nose.

Approved July 20, 1976

Reformatted November 28, 1990

THE KENNEL CLUB STANDARD FOR THE BULLDOG

General Appearance—Smooth-coated, thick set, rather low in stature, broad, powerful and compact. Head, fairly large in proportion to size but no point so much in excess of others as to destroy the general symmetry, or make the dog appear deformed, or interfere with its powers of motion. Face short, muzzle broad, blunt and inclined upwards. Dogs showing respiratory distress highly undesirable. Body short, well knit, limbs stout, well muscled and in hard condition with no tendency towards obesity. Hindquarters high and strong but somewhat lighter in comparison with heavy foreparts. Bitches not so grand or well developed as dogs.

Characteristics—Conveys impression of determination, strength and activity.

Temperament—Alert, bold, loyal, dependable, courageous, fierce in appearance, but possessed of affectionate nature.

Head and Skull—Skull large in circumference. Viewed from front appears very high from corner of lower jaw to apex of skull; also very broad and square. Cheeks well rounded and extended sideways beyond

Coat color varies from dog to dog. Brindle is the preferred coat color.

eyes. Viewed from side, head appears very high and short from back to point of nose. Forehead flat with skin upon and about head, loose and wrinkled, neither prominent nor overhanging face. Projections of frontal bones prominent, broad, square and high; deep, wide indentation between eyes. From stop, a furrow, both broad and deep extending to middle of skull being traceable to apex. Face from front of cheek bone to nose, short, skin wrinkled. Muzzle short, broad, turned upwards and very deep from corner of eye to corner of mouth. Nose and nostrils large, broad and black, under no circumstances liver colour, red or brown; top set back towards eyes. Distance from inner corner of eye (or from centre of stop between eyes) to extreme tip of nose not exceeding length from tip of nose to edge of underlip. Nostrils large wide and open, with well defined vertical straight line between. Flews (chops) thick, broad, pendant and very deep, hanging completely over lower jaws at sides, not in front, joining underlip in front and quite covering teeth. Jaws broad, massive and square, lower jaw projecting in front of upper and turning up. Nose roll must not interfere with the line of layback. Viewed from front, the various properties of the face must be equally balanced on either side of an imaginary line down centre.

Eyes—Seen from front, situated low down in skull, well away from ears. Eyes and stop in same straight line, at right angles to furrow. Wide apart, but outer corners within the outline of cheeks. Round in shape, of moderate size, neither sunken nor prominent, in colour very dark—almost black—showing no white when looking directly forward. Free from obvious eye problems.

Ears—Set high—i.e. front edge of each ear (as viewed from front) joins outline of skull at top corner of such outline, so as to place them as wide apart, as high and as far from eyes as possible. Small and thin. 'Rose ear' correct, i.e. folding inwards back, upper or front inner edge curving outwards and backwards, showing part of inside of burr.

Mouth—Jaws broad and square with six small front teeth between canines in an even row. Canines wide apart. Teeth large and strong, not seen when mouth closed. When viewed from front under jaw directly under upper jaw and parallel.

Neck—Moderate in length, very thick, deep and strong. Well arched at back, with much loose, thick and wrinkled skin about throat, forming dewlap on each side, from lower jaw to chest.

Forequarters—Shoulders broad, sloping and deep, very powerful and muscular giving appearance of being 'tacked on' body. Brisket capacious, round and very deep from top of shoulders to lowest part where it joins chest. Well let down between forelegs. Large in diameter, round behind forelegs (not flat-sided, ribs well rounded). Forelegs very stout and strong, well developed, set wide apart, thick, muscular and straight, presenting rather bowed outline, but bones of legs large and straight, not bandy nor curved and short in proportion to hindlegs, but

The Bulldog's tail may be straight or "screwed." The screwed tail (shown here) should have well-defined bends or kinks and no portion should be elevated above the base or root.

not so short as to make back appear long, or detract from dog's activity and so cripple him. Elbows low and standing well away from ribs. Pasterns short, straight and strong.

Body—Chest wide, laterally round, prominent and deep. Back short, strong, broad at shoulders, comparatively narrower at loins. Slight fall to back close behind shoulders (lowest part) whence spine should rise to loins (top higher than top of shoulder), curving again more suddenly to tail, forming arch (termed roach back)—a distinctive characteristic of breed. Body well ribbed up behind with belly tucked up and not pendulous.

Hindquarters—Legs large and muscular, longer in proportion than forelegs, so as to elevate loins. Hocks slightly bent, well let down; legs long and muscular from loins to hock; short, straight, strong lower part. Stifles round and turned slightly outwards away from body. Hocks thereby made to approach each other and hind feet to turn outwards.

Feet—Fore, straight and turning very slightly outward; of medium size and moderately round. Hind, round and compact. Toes compact and thick, well split up, making knuckles prominent and high.

Tail—Set on low, jutting out rather straight and then turning downwards. Round, smooth and devoid of fringe or coarse hair. Moderate in length—rather short than long—thick at root, tapering quickly to a fine point. Downward carriage (not having a decided upward curve at end) and never carried above back.

Gait/Movement—Peculiarly heavy and constrained, appearing to walk with short, quick steps on tips of toes, hind feet not lifted high, appearing to skim ground, running with one or other shoulder rather advanced. Soundness of movement of the utmost importance.

Coat—Fine texture, short, close and smooth (hard only from shortness and closeness, not wiry).

Colour—Whole or smut, (i.e. whole colour with black mask or muzzle). Only whole colours (which should be brilliant and pure of their sort) viz., brindles, reds with their various shades, fawns, fallows etc., white and pied (i.e. combination of white with any of the foregoing colours). Dudley, black and black with tan highly undesirable.

Size—Dogs: 25 kgs (55 lbs); bitches: 23 kgs (50 lbs).

Faults—Any departure from the foregoing points should be considered a fault and the seriousness with which the fault should be regarded should be in exact proportion to its degree and its effect upon the health and welfare of the dog.

Note—Male animals should have two apparently normal testicles fully descended into the scrotum.

September 2000

Selecting Your Bulldog

So you want to become a Bulldogger, do you? Prepare to enter a rare and wonderful world of humans peculiarly devoted to their burly buddies. Of course, first you have to find that perfect little Bulldog puppy, and finding a Bulldog isn't always an easy task. Finding a Bulldog bred by a responsi-

Make sure that the Bulldog is the right one for you. Research your options before making a final decision.

ble and ethical breeder actively breeding for good temperament and health can be even more challenging, but well worth the effort.

Just how do you find such breeders, and once you do, how will you know it? What should you look for in a Bulldog puppy? Which one should you choose?

WHO'S BREEDING MY BULLY?

The first step in locating a healthy, happy Bulldog puppy is to locate a Bulldog breeder who is breeding healthy, happy Bulldog puppies. While you can probably find a Bulldog breeder willing to sell you a puppy, how will you know you've located a good one? Responsible Bulldog breeders are in the business for the love of Bullies, not the money. Breeding Bulldogs is very costly, and even though a reputable Bulldog breeder's puppies may seem expensive to you, rest assured the Bulldog breeder is probably just barely recovering costs. Because of their large heads and narrow hips, female Bulldogs usually require cesarean sections, which in themselves are very expensive. Add to that cost the care of the mother, vet visits for all the puppies, initial vaccinations, worming, skin care, and the constant monitoring and attention mother and puppies require, and you will see that the breeder is pouring many resources into the care of those little Bulldog pups.

Before making your selection, visit several reputable breeders.

Reputable and responsible Bulldog breeders are usually show breeders trying to earn the title of "Champion" on their most promising prospects. They then look for appropriate pet homes for those dogs that don't quite match the breed standard but would nevertheless make excellent pets.

Show breeders work hard to preserve the best characteristics of Bulldogs. Puppies are most likely to be healthy, well cared for, and well socialized from birth. Responsible Bulldog breeders breed with purpose and forethought. They study the breed standard and learn all about health, canine genetics, and Bulldog care. They are most likely to learn about

When you visit the breeder, ask him lots of questions. Find out as much as you can about the dam and sire of the litter.

advances in canine genetics and keep their dogs up-to-date with all appropriate genetic tests in order to avoid passing on genetic problems. When responsible breeders do produce Bulldogs with genetic problems, they typically have them spayed or neutered and removed from their breeding programs.

Breeders who don't know much about Bulldog genetics, proper Bulldog hygiene, or puppy socialization and training are less likely to be breeding with these important considerations in mind. Avoid breeders only looking to make a profit, as well as those who can't or won't show you either of a puppy's parents. Also avoid breeders who try to, or are willing to, sell you a puppy younger than eight weeks old. The first eight weeks (or even a couple of weeks longer) are essential for Bulldog puppies to get the full social benefits of life with the mother and littermates. Do your research and you'll be rewarded with the very best Bulldog puppy you can get.

Choosing a good breeder also means you will have support, advice, and encouragement throughout the life of your Bulldog. You should be able to call the breeder with problems and questions, even five years from now. And, responsible breeders will always agree to take your Bulldog back if you should ever find yourself unable to keep him.

Of course, finding that perfect breeder can be challenging, so keep the following considerations in mind when researching, visiting, and interviewing Bulldog breeders:

- Don't go with the first Bulldog breeder you meet. He or she might be the best one around, but comparison shopping will teach you a lot about different kinds of situations, kennels, conditions, and breeders.
- Get recommendations. Ask around. Visit dog shows. Talk to owners of Bulldogs you admire. Call the breeder referral contact person for the Bulldog Club of America (www.thebca.org). Do as much research as you can and ask people which Bulldog breeders in your area or region are breeding Bulldogs that make excellent pets.
- Pay an initial visit to a breeder but don't buy a puppy right away. A preliminary visit to a breeder can tell you a lot, both about the breeder and about the conditions in which the dogs are kept. Are the Bulldogs living inside? Do they look healthy and happy? Is the facility reasonably clean?
- Ask the breeder questions about Bulldogs, and be wary if you only hear good things, or if the breeder tries to pressure you into buying a puppy right then and there. A responsible breeder will be just as choosy about you as you should be about him or her , and will probably subject you to a lengthy interview. This is a good thing. It means the breeder is breeding with the best interests of the Bulldogs in mind.
- Ask the breeder if he or she shows the dogs and how many championships dogs from the breeder's lines have earned. Ask to see some of the puppies' pedigrees, or if the litter isn't yet born, the parents' pedigrees. A pedigree is a record of the dog's lineage for at least three generations back. In the pedigree, those dogs that have earned championships have a "Ch." title before their names. Remember that unless you plan to show your Bulldog, you don't need a potential champion. However, knowing the breeder puts time and effort into breeding dogs that could be champions is evidence that he or she is working hard to produce the very best Bulldogs (even if your particular puppy doesn't have quite the right ear set, shoulder angle, or underbite!).
- Ask the breeder for references, both from the breeder's vet and from people who have purchased puppies previously. Actually check the references. A vet in particular can tell you a lot about the health of that breeder's lines. If the breeder refuses to give you any references, look elsewhere for your puppy.

When looking for a show dog, familiarize yourself with the breed standard.

- Ask to see the parents, or at least the mother, of the litter. Some breeders breed to sires (fathers of the litter) belonging to other breeders, but they should at least be willing to show you the dam (mother).
- Do the parents look like the kind of Bulldog you want to have? Are they friendly and relaxed, or anxious, hyperactive, nervous, shy, or aggressive? Many physical and temperamental traits are inherited, so the parents should look and act essentially how you would like your own Bully to look and act. This still, however, does not guarantee that your dog will have a similar temperament to his parents.
- Consider driving a few miles, even into a different state, if you don't have good show breeders in your area. It will be worth the trip. Also consider putting your name on a waiting list instead of buying from breeders who have puppies *right now.* A good puppy is worth the wait.
- Trust your instincts. If you feel you are communicating well with a breeder, find that he or she takes good care of the dogs and explains both the joys and challenges of living with and caring for a Bulldog, and experience a general sense of trust, then you have probably found a good breeder. If you have misgivings about the conditions or the information the breeder is giving you, if you feel pressured, or simply feel uneasy or don't trust what the breeder is telling you, don't feel obligated to buy anything. Thank the breeder and keep looking. Or, say you'll think about it, and leave the premises to give it more thought. Don't rush into the purchase of a puppy that will be a part of the family for years to come.

HOW TO PICK A PUPPY

Once you've settled on a breeder you feel good about, you can begin the process of choosing a puppy. If you have to be on a waiting list, use this time to research Bulldog health, care, and training. When it's finally time to get your puppy, you may think you know exactly which one you want, but wait! Nobody knows the litter better than the breeder, who has been carefully handling, socializing, and watching the individual puppies.

The breeder should have a good idea about which puppies are more docile, which are more outgoing, and which might best fit into your particular situation. He or she can advise you on which puppy would make a good match for you. Of course, sometimes you can't argue with chemistry. The Bulldog puppy that climbs into your lap (and heart) and settles right in comfortably may indeed be the perfect puppy for you.

Of course, the puppy you choose should look healthy and curious,

If you are looking for a family pet as opposed to a show dog, choose the pup that is the most eager to be with you.

friendly and outgoing, not shy, sickly, or unusually low on energy. A mellow puppy that wants to cuddle isn't the same as a puppy that seems unable to fully wake up or that doesn't want to move at all (unless it's naptime, of course). The puppy's skin should be in good condition with no bare patches or infected areas. Eyes should be bright, clear, and clean, and the puppy's nose, ears, and rear end should be clean and free of discharge. The puppy should also be able to breathe easily, although all Bulldogs tend to snort and snore.

Along with your puppy, you should receive:

- A receipt.
- A sales contract.
- A copy of the puppy's pedigree for at least three generations.
- A copy of the puppy's medical records indicating the worming and immunizations already performed.
- A registration application or signed registration certificate so you can register your Bulldog. (For a pet, the breeder will likely give you the paperwork to do a limited registration, which means you can register your dog but not breed him or her.)
- A health guarantee. (This may be part of the sales contract.)
- Instructions on feeding and care, and in many cases, a small amount of the food the puppy has already been eating.

HEALTH GUARANTEES, CONTRACTS, AND OTHER RED TAPE

The paperwork involved in buying a puppy may seem like an annoyance. You want to get your Bully home! However, these documents are important, both for your own and the breeder's protection.

A sales contract/health guarantee should specify in exacting terms what is expected of you, what is expected of the breeder, and in what cases the

Although your Bulldog may have a pedigree, he may not be a show dog.

dog can be returned for a full, partial, or no refund. For instance, you may be required to take your Bulldog to a vet within 48 hours for a checkup, but if the vet finds a health problem, you can return the puppy for a full refund. The contract might also state that any health problems arising that are genetic or due to care while the puppy was with the breeder justify a refund, but that health problems or accidents that occur due to your care or through no fault of the breeder do not justify a refund. Look for a clause that states the breeder will take the Bulldog back at any time during his life if you are unable to keep him. Some contracts require that you return the Bulldog rather than relinquish him to a shelter or rescue group.

Bulldogs tend to have a number of health problems, most related to their short faces, wrinkled skin, and other genetic aspects. Some you may be willing to deal with, and some you must actively work to avoid (such as keeping skin wrinkles clean and keeping the dog from overheating). In the case of certain genetic conditions, such as heart problems or hip dysplasia, the breeder may agree to pay for part of the treatment if you want to keep the dog. The contract may also require that you have the dog spayed or neutered, that you promise not to breed the dog, or if you are planning on entering the world of breeding and showing (think long and hard about this arduous and sometimes heartbreaking undertaking), the breeder may require that you give him or her the first pick of the litter.

Be sure to read the whole contract. Obviously, once you sign, you are agreeing to those conditions, and you may have a tough time and no legal rights to change your mind later. Until you sign, however, you can always change your mind, and it is better to decide not to take home a Bulldog puppy than to go ahead, not sure if you really want to be responsible for the high level of care and attention a Bulldog will require for the next 8 to 12 years. If you are sure that you are meant to be a Bulldogger and the contract is agreeable to you, sign away and take that wrinkly, roly-poly little Bulldog puppy home.

ADOPTING A RESCUED BULLDOG

Some people would rather adopt an adult Bulldog than a puppy. Sometimes, breeders have adult Bulldogs that need homes. These dogs can be happy, well-trained, well-socialized pet prospects that are wrapping up a show career or didn't quite turn out, conformationally, the way the breeder had hoped. If you want to avoid housetraining, puppy teething, and the other aspects of puppy ownership, an adult Bulldog may be your best bet.

Another source for adult Bulldogs is Bulldog rescue. Bulldog rescue networks, both national and local, take in abandoned, relinquished, or otherwise homeless Bulldogs, evaluate them for temperament and health, and try to place them in appropriate homes. Some rescued Bulldogs are already well-trained family pets. Others have suffered abuse, abandonment, or have a basic lack of socialization and/or training. These Bulldogs require work, patience, more work, and more patience. They are not usually good bets for homes with children unless the rescue workers know they have been raised with and are comfortable with children. The dogs may be fearful, shy, or aggressive, and they may not trust people. Consider adopting a Bulldog as similar to adopting a child: Some have more problems than others, but of course, the ones with problems desperately need someone willing to commit to rehabilitation.

If you are interested in adopting a Bulldog, talk to your local or regional rescue coordinator about your situation. You may need to wait a short while or a long while for a Bulldog that will fit into your home, but stay in touch with the rescue group (you might even decide to volunteer your services), and when the right Bully comes along, you'll be ready. Another option is to foster rescued Bulldogs

Remember that your choice is not just limited to puppies. There are thousands of adult Bulldogs available through rescue agencies and your local animal shelter.

until the rescue group can find permanent homes.

For more information on Bulldog rescue, check out the Bulldog Club of America rescue page online at www.rescuebulldogs.org/. The link to their Rescue Roster will list individual rescue contacts all over the US.

SHOPPING SPREE

Bulldogs need certain supplies and equipment. Shop before bringing home your Bulldog puppy so you can have a cozy den, food and water in clean bowls, a collar and leash, and chew toys all ready to go.

Take this list to the pet store to stock up for your Bulldog:

- A nylon or leather buckle collar and 6-foot leash. Lightweight nylon may be more comfortable for your puppy that will be new to the concept of collars and leashes. Nylon may also be more adjustable and less expensive to replace as your Bulldog grows. You can always upgrade to leather when your Bulldog is full-grown.
- A high-quality, premium puppy food.
- Food and water bowls, preferably metal or ceramic, which your Bully can't chew.
- Chew toys! Bulldog puppies need to chew and require lots of fun, interactive toys to keep them busy. Avoid chew toys like rawhide bones that could break off into pieces, which could choke a Bulldog. Chew toys like Nylabones® are safer for Bulldogs.
- Toys for play. Bulldogs enjoy playing with toys, carrying them around, and collecting them. Interactive toys can also keep a Bulldog puppy's mind busy. Bulldogs enjoy stuffable toys, which can be filled with kibble. To release the "treat," the Bulldog must manipulate the toy in the right way.
- A crate. Bulldog puppies feel safe and comfortable in a cozy crate, where they can relax away from the chaos once in awhile. A crate, such as a Nylabone® Fold-Away Pet Carrier, will also help to housetrain your Bully. Cover the crate with a cozy blanket, cushion, or fleece mat.
- A soft, natural-bristle brush for grooming. Bulldogs shed, but a once-over with a brush every few days will keep shedding to a minimum.

BRINGING YOUR BULLY HOME

At last, you can bring your new Bully puppy home with you. This is an exciting time for everyone in the family, but don't forget to give your Bully time to rest on his own, lots of cuddling and attention, and a solid start at learning household rules, including housetraining. Take good care of your new Bully, and soon you'll be hooked, well on your way to calling yourself a full-fledged "Bulldogger."

Feeding Your Bulldog

Bulldogs love to eat, and feeding a Bulldog the right way is one of the best means of keeping your roly-poly puppy or adult dog in good shape, with a shiny coat, good digestion, and just the right amount of muscle and body fat. All Bulldogs need good nutrition to stay healthy and just enough calories to avoid becoming overweight.

Feeding your Bulldog can be confusing when you survey the many brands of puppy and dog food on the pet store shelves. Should you feed kibble or canned food? Which brand, how much, and how often? Should you add people food or not?

Actually, feeding a Bulldog isn't all that complicated if you know some basics. Read on to find out the best way to keep your Bulldog healthy by providing the very best diet. Remember, what your dog eats is up to you, so your Bulldog's health is largely in your hands.

The amount of food fed and the number of time a day you feed your Bulldog will change as he ages.

BULLY NUTRITION 101

All dogs need certain vitamins and minerals as well as protein and fat in their diets. Fortunately, scientists understand exactly what most dogs need, and pet food companies use that information in formulating pet foods. Unless you plan to feed your Bulldog a homemade diet, you can trust that a quality pet food will supply your Bulldog with all the essential components of a healthy diet.

As for supplements and added foods, if your breeder uses them, you should keep up the same schedule, at least for the first few weeks. Most veterinarians agree that most dogs don't really need vitamin, mineral, or herbal supplements if they are eating a high-quality, balanced diet. Yet, some breeders and veterinarians think certain breeds can benefit from certain kinds of supplements. Talk to your breeder and vet if you want to give your Bulldog a supplement, and get their approval first.

The Bulldog Club of America suggests the occasional addition of cottage cheese, nonfat yogurt, and/or corn or canola oil to a Bulldog puppy's food to help grow strong bones, encourage good digestion, and maintain a shiny, healthy coat. These additions are optional, but Bulldogs certainly enjoy this healthy form of pampering. While dogs probably don't need any variety in their diets, feeding them a varied diet with any changes made gradually over the period of a week or two will be easiest on your Bulldog's digestion.

Choose a dog food that meets your Bulldog's needs. Table scraps and other people foods should be limited or given as rewards for good behavior.

Of course, all dogs need an ample supply of clean, fresh water. Because Bulldogs get easily overheated, this is particularly important. Be sure the water bowl is big enough for your Bulldog to drink from easily.

Finally, remember that because of their flat faces and skin wrinkles, Bulldogs can get pretty messy when eating and drinking. They snort, snuffle, and spray. Their jowls drip after a good long drink of water, and food can even get into those wrinkles, so make sure the Bulldog's face stays clean and dry to prevent skin irritation. Bulldogs have sensitive skin, and even certain kinds of food bowls can cause irritation or rashes. Stick to metal or ceramic, which are more sterile. Metal is also unbreakable and the preferred choice among Bulldog breeders. Also, due to a Bulldog's flat face, the bowl should have a flat bottom and straight sides so he can easily get to the food. Having a mug like that can be a challenge!

FEEDING YOUR BULLDOG PUPPY

Bulldog puppies need a high-quality puppy food so they can grow strong bones and muscles and develop a healthy skin and coat. Because puppies have smaller stomachs and quicker digestion, they need to eat more often than adults. Until your Bulldog puppy is about three months old, he should eat four small meals a day. Divide up the daily allowance of food into four separate parts (reserving some of it for training, too, rather than adding extra treats).

It is fine to give your Bulldog the occasional treat as long as it is nutritious and does not upset his regular meals.

Between four and six months, you can reduce feeding to three times per day, and after six months, two meals a day. Each time, take the total amount of food for the day and divide by the appropriate number of meals so they become fewer but larger. Keep an eye on your Bull to make sure he isn't overweight. Puppies should be round and fat, but you should be able to feel (not see) their ribs when running your hands along your Bulldog's sides.

Bulldog puppies need plenty of food, but not so much that they get *too* roly-poly. Follow the directions on the food bag for how much food your puppy needs each day. Most dog foods have a chart listing a range for puppies of a certain weight and age. For instance, your puppy food might say that puppies between 8 and 12 pounds should have 1 to 2 cups of food per day. Start on the low end of the range to avoid overfeeding. If you are feeding three meals a day of this particular food, give your Bulldog puppy 1/3 cup at each meal. Then, if your Bulldog puppy starts to look too thin, you can gradually increase the amount. If your Bulldog puppy starts to look too fat, decrease the amount slightly. Your vet can help you to determine whether your Bulldog is growing at a healthy rate and maintaining a healthy weight.

WHICH FOOD IS BEST?

Walking into the dog food aisle at a pet store can be overwhelming. So many brands, so many types! Which should you choose for your Bulldog? Canned or kibble? Premium or super-premium? Organic? Holistic? Or is the cheapest brand on the shelf just as good as the most expensive?

Fresh, clean water is just as important to healthy nutrition as is food.

The answers to many of these questions depend on whom you ask, but generally, premium foods contain higher-quality ingredients than budget foods and will be less likely to cause digestive and skin problems in your Bulldog. "Premium" pet foods or "super-premium" pet foods usually cost more than less-expensive foods, but make up for that price difference in three ways: decreased stool volume, smaller feeding amounts (so the bag lasts longer), and typically, higher levels of protein. These high-quality foods may also help to keep your Bulldog's sensitive skin healthy, but a teaspoon of corn, canola, or flaxseed oil on your Bulldog's food each day can boost skin health even more.

Check the label of your pet food to see if meat or meat meal (including lamb, chicken, beef, and turkey) are listed among the first four ingredients. The more meat products at the top of the list the better. Also check the Guaranteed Analysis. A quality pet food should have at least 25 percent protein. Naturally preserved foods and foods that contain other healthy ingredients like vegetables, fruits, and whole grains may also help your Bulldog to get all the vitamins and minerals he needs. Some

Puppies require a different type of food than older dogs. Consult your veterinarian or breeder for suggestions on which type should be fed to your Bulldog.

Bulldogs don't react well to soy, so avoid foods with soybeans in the ingredients list.

Because of their flat faces, Bulldogs can make a mess of a bowl of canned food! They love the taste, however. Some people mix a small amount of canned food into dry kibble for palatability, but this isn't necessary. Choose a premium or super-premium canned food, also. If your Bulldog starts to have skin problems, eliminate canned food to see if that helps.

WHAT ABOUT HOMEMADE DIETS?

For some Bulldoggers, only the highest-quality human foods will do for their pampered Bulldogs, but making your own pet food isn't easy. Most pet owners don't have the time or inclination to do the extra work, gain the extra knowledge, and commit to the careful preparation required for a homemade diet, but others believe it is the best way to keep their Bulldogs healthy.

The problem with homemade diets is that you have to know exactly what to put in them to prevent nutritional deficiencies in your Bulldog. A bowl of meat twice a day won't provide your Bulldog with everything he needs. Bulldogs need the vitamins, minerals, and other nutritional components of meat, grains, and vegetables in just the right proportions.

Certain foods can be toxic to Bulldogs, or can at least cause digestive or allergic problems. Avoid soy, grapes, onions, and chocolate. Also,

Chew toys, such as those made by Nylabone®, will keep your Bulldog busy. They will also help to keep your dog from overeating.

highly processed, fatty, salty "people food" isn't any better for your Bulldog than it is for you. Just because he looks at you with "that face" is no excuse. He doesn't need it!

Advising you on exactly how to prepare a homemade diet is beyond the scope of this book, but if you would like to try it, talk to your breeder and your veterinarian, then do some research. Many books will tell you how to make a homemade diet.

PREVENTING OBESITY

Veterinarians claim that the number-one health problem in pets today is obesity. With their round figures, couch-potato tendencies, and love of a good meal, Bulldogs are at risk for becoming overweight. Unfortunately, too much weight on your Bulldog puts him at risk for many health problems. Excess weight makes breathing more difficult, a task that can already be a challenge for the flat-faced Bulldog. It also puts a strain on your Bulldog's heart and joints and can aggravate arthritis in his senior years.

Keeping your Bulldog from becoming overweight is easy! Stick to a sensible amount of food, feeding your adult Bulldog twice a day so he can enjoy mealtime more often. Limit treats, especially high-fat, heavily processed treats. Instead, use a portion of your Bulldog's regular kibble for training, or give him small amounts of healthy treats, such as freeze-dried liver, small bits of lean meat and cheese, even soft fruits and vegetables like blueberries and cooked carrots if your Bulldog likes them. (Avoid grapes, which can be toxic for some dogs, and small pieces of hard food like raw carrots, which can pose a choking hazard.)

Keep an eye on your Bulldog and remember to check his sides periodically. If you can feel, but not see, those ribs then your Bulldog is probably just fine. If your veterinarian says your Bulldog is getting too heavy, however, follow your vet's advice for scaling back portions or switching to a high-quality weight-loss formula food.

Grooming Your Bulldog

Bulldogs may not look much like Poodles or other breeds people typically associate with fancy grooming, but they need grooming nevertheless. Grooming your Bulldog is an important part of keeping him healthy. His sensitive skin, shedding coat, and skin wrinkles need special attention, and just as with any dog, regular grooming will keep you in touch with and aware of your Bulldog's physical condition.

Fortunately, Bulldogs are among the easiest dogs to groom because of their short, hard coats. While daily grooming isn't necessary, it does go quickly and can benefit you and your Bulldog by minimizing the effects of hair shedding and giving you the opportunity to keep an eye on potential skin irritation or other problems. A quick brushing and rubdown every morning after you finish your own grooming routine can become a healthy and enjoyable habit for both you and your Bulldog.

This Bulldog is enjoying a thorough brushing. Make sure that the brush you use is kept clean.

BRUSHING YOUR BULLDOG

Bulldogs don't have to contend with tangles and mats, but regular brushing can keep the effects of shedding to a minimum. Bulldog hair is short, stiff, and weaves itself into furniture, carpets, and clothing. It isn't easy to get out, either. A daily brushing will make a big difference in the amount of hair let loose into your home, but for those pressed for time, a thorough brushing two or three times a week should be sufficient to keep your Bulldog's coat in good condition.

Because Bulldogs have such sensitive skin and short coats, they require only a very soft bristle brush or rubber curry comb. Avoid slicker brushes, pin brushes, and other brushes with stiff or wire bristles, as these can cause brush burn and other skin irritation. Brush your Bulldog in an area that is easy to clean up, such as a bathroom with a tile floor, on a counter or grooming table, or outside.

Begin at the base of your Bulldog's tail, and brush against the natural lay of hair in order to loosen dead hair. Work your way all over the body, up the legs, and gently around the head, ears, and face. Don't forget to brush your Bulldog's underside. Then, brush your Bulldog with the lay of hair, smoothing the coat. Finally, rub your Bulldog all over with your hands to stimulate the skin's natural oil production. This will keep your dog's coat shiny and sleek and will also alert you to any lumps, bumps, rashes, or other skin changes.

Excessive bathing can dry out your Bulldog's skin. Make sure you thoroughly rinse your dog's coat to remove all soap residue.

A Bulldog is a sight to behold. When properly groomed, the Bulldog makes quite an impression in the show ring.

BATHING YOUR BULLDOG

Bulldogs don't need many baths, and in fact, too much bathing can dry out the Bulldog's skin. Bathe your Bulldog only when he gets dirty. The bathtub, the kitchen sink, or a washtub in the yard will all make suitable bathing spots. Put a nylon collar on your Bulldog before bathing in order to hold on to him and keep him from jumping out of the tub.

Next, ready your supplies. These are the things you will need to bathe your Bulldog:

- A mild shampoo made for dogs. Some of these enhance your Bulldog's natural color and are designed to brighten white coats, add depth to black coats, or enhance red coats.
- A conditioner. This can help keep dry hair looking healthy.
- Cotton balls.
- Mineral oil or eye ointment.
- Petroleum jelly.
- A soft bathing brush.
- A large towel.

Run the water into the tub or sink. Be sure the water isn't too hot. Secure your Bulldog by holding his collar or attaching his collar and leash to a secure fixture. Put a cotton ball in each ear and put a drop of mineral oil or eye ointment in each eye. Wet your Bulldog's coat using a sprayer attachment or a cup. Be sure to wet the entire coat, including the underside.

Next, rub some shampoo between your palms and then over your

Bulldog's entire coat. Using your hands or the bathing brush, work the shampoo down to the skin. Be sure to get inside all those skin wrinkles where dirt and bacteria often lie hidden. Wash your Bulldog's paw pads and between his toes, around his eyes, and in all the wrinkles around his nose and mouth. Then wash his nose, belly, genitals, and under his tail.

Rinse your Bulldog thoroughly. Any remaining shampoo in those skin wrinkles can cause irritation. Apply a coat conditioner, then towel-dry your Bulldog. Be sure to dry all those wrinkles because leftover moisture can also encourage bacteria growth. Your Bulldog's coat will still be wet even after he has been towel dried, so keep him inside until his coat is completely dry. Otherwise, he could become chilled or might just feel the need for a good roll in the dirt (and then you'll have to start all over again!).

BULLDOG MANICURE

Unless your Bulldog makes a habit of walking on concrete, you will need to trim his nails about every two weeks. A Bulldog resistant to nail trimming can be a difficult customer, so begin regular nail trimming on young puppies so they become accustomed to the procedure. You should use nail trimmers made for dogs, either guillotine or scissors style, and they should be very sharp or they will pull on the nail, making the process uncomfortable for the dog.

The most important thing to remember in trimming your Bulldog's nails is

By beginning to trim your Bulldog's nails when he's a puppy, he will become accustomed to this as part of his grooming sessions and not be afraid.

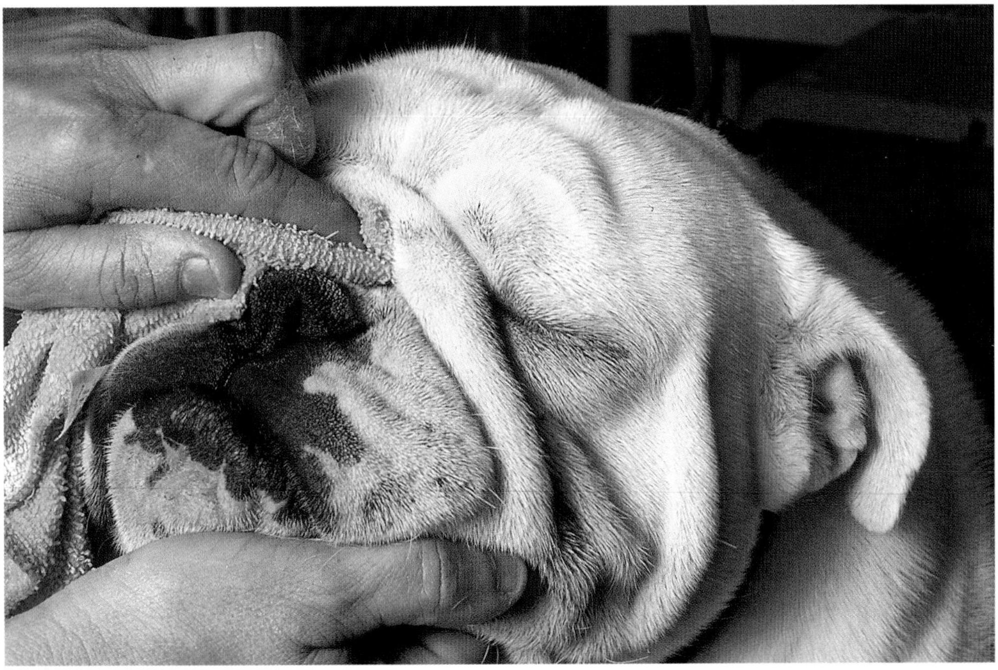

Your Bulldog's nose and facial wrinkles should be cleaned on a daily basis to lessen the bacterial and yeast accumulation that could cause infection.

to avoid cutting the quick, which is the vein that runs partway down your Bulldog's nail. In white nails, the quick is easy to see, but in black nails, don't cut beyond the curved tip. If you cut the quick, it will bleed and be painful for your dog. Have a styptic pencil or other coagulating powder handy, just in case. Clipping the quick is a fast way to turn your Bulldog against nail trimming, so be careful; if it happens, though, don't make a big deal about it and your Bulldog won't either. Stop the bleeding and try again later.

Regular nail trimming (every two weeks) will encourage the quick to recede farther back into the nail. Trimming infrequently encourages the quick to extend out farther, so make regular nail trimming a habit. Untrimmed nails can also put your Bulldog at risk for foot injuries because the nails force the paw pads to splay out unnaturally. Bulldog nails should be short and blunt.

Nail clippers leave the nail tip rough, so after clipping, file each nail tip until it is smooth. Or, use a nail grinder (like a dremel tool) to keep nails smooth and short. Expose your Bulldog to the nail grinder a little at a time so it doesn't startle him. Also be careful not to grind into the quick, just as you would be careful not to clip it.

BULLDOG DETAILING

Now that your Bulldog is nicely brushed, squeaky-clean, and manicured, a few finishing touches will make him truly the picture of the well-

After playing outside, especially in tall grass, Bulldogs need to be inspected for bugs and parasites that may cause any number of diseases.

groomed English gentleman. Polish and moisten your Bulldog's nose and nails with just a dab of petroleum jelly. Clean out his ears with a cotton swab, removing any visible wax. Keep baby wipes with aloe and lanolin handy to clean skin wrinkles between baths, and use a tear-stain-removing product to keep the eye area free of stains (a common problem on light-colored Bulldogs). Ask your breeder or local pet store about the best products for removing tear stains and for keeping the under-eye area clean and dry to prevent re-staining.

Now isn't he handsome?

NO FLEAS, PLEASE

Fleas are no fun, and their effects on the Bulldog's sensitive skin can be devastating. If your Bulldog is rarely exposed to fleas, prevent an infestation through frequent brushing. Keep a watchful eye for signs of fleas: black specks (flea eggs), red specks (digested blood), or the tiny jumping rascals themselves. The Bulldog's short coat makes fleas easy to spot, especially on light-colored Bulldogs. Treat any sign of fleas immediately.

In some climates, such as in the southern US, fleas are hard to avoid. Some Bulldogs are allergic to flea saliva, and just a few fleabites can turn into a major skin problem with itching, hot spots, and infection. Flea shampoos can be harsh, but may be necessary on occasion. Avoid flea collars and other potent chemicals unless your vet recommends them. The monthly spot-on products are generally well tolerated and are a great way to prevent flea infestations in the first place in areas where fleas are a problem. Purchase these from your veterinarian. These products come in monthly doses, applied between the shoulder blades. They move over the skin and kill fleas on contact for a full month. Some products also protect against ticks and heartworm. Your vet can recommend the best product for your dog that is most appropriate for your area of the country.

If your Bulldog does develop fleabite dermatitis or flea allergies, don't wait to treat the problem. Itchy skin and hot spots are no fun for your Bulldog. Your veterinarian can recommend the right products to treat your Bulldog's skin problem.

Training Your Bulldog

Bulldogs can be as stubborn as they look, but that doesn't mean they can't become well-trained, well-behaved family members. All dogs need training to understand household rules. Training is simply a way to establish communication between you and your Bulldog.

However, training a Bulldog isn't as easy as repeating an exercise hundreds of times until your Bulldog does it reliably. Bulldogs like to please you...to a point. But if they lose interest or the motivation isn't strong enough or they simply don't want to do something, they can be a challenge. The trick to training a Bulldog is to make the experience so fun, rewarding, and interesting that he can't imagine wanting to do anything other than follow your requests.

HOUSETRAINING YOUR BULLY

Bulldogs aren't difficult to housetrain, as long as they understand what you want them to do and as long as your training methods fall in line with their

Train your Bulldog to relieve himself outside.

natural habits and behaviors. The key to quick and successful housetraining is to *never let your Bully make a mistake.* Sure, we all miss a cue sometimes and have to clean up a puppy puddle, but the more times your Bully relieves himself in the *right* spot and the less often he relieves himself in the *wrong* spot, the faster he will learn what you expect of him.

You can accomplish this teaching process easily by combining two of the most popular housetraining methods at the same time: crate training, and schedule training.

Crate Training

Crate training involves using a plastic or metal crate where your Bully can rest when you can't supervise him in those early weeks. Whenever you are not watching him for signs that he needs to go outside, put him in his crate. For this reason, you should be around often when you first get your puppy because young puppies don't have good bladder control and they need to relieve themselves often.

Select a crate that will be large enough to house your dog when he's fully grown. The Nylabone® Fold-Away Pet Carrier is recommended by veterinarians and breeders alike. It sets up easily and folds down quickly when necessary. It also makes a great home for your pet.

Crate training doesn't mean throwing your Bully puppy in his crate and leaving him there for hours on end. In fact, this kind of practice is antithetical to crate training because it will set your Bully up for failure and result in negative associations with the crate. Instead, the crate (or let's call it a den, which sounds like a much nicer word and more descriptive of the crate's purpose) should become a place of comfort and a cozy, safe haven for your Bully puppy. The den can be the place your Bully goes when he needs a break from chaos, needs to rest and cool off after an active play session (put a pan of ice in there with him to help him cool off and give him something to chew), or simply a place to take a nice nap. Dogs naturally gravitate towards covered spaces like the crate because they feel safe and secure inside these spaces.

Crate training works because, unless they have a medical problem, most dogs won't soil where they sleep (unless left in the crate for too long—puppies have their limits). Make sure the den is soft and comfortable. A fleece mat or folded blanket (or both) makes the den inviting and pleasant. The den should be just big enough for your Bully puppy to stand up, turn around, lie down, and stretch out, but not so big that he can relieve himself in one corner and sleep in another corner. Train your Bully puppy to enjoy his den by putting him inside the very first day you bring him home, but leaving him in it for only short periods of time at first. He may whine, cry, and paw at the bars. Reassure him in a comforting voice, but don't be swayed to "rescue" him. He doesn't need rescuing; he just needs to learn the rules. Give him a few treats or a special chew toy he only gets to have in his crate.

Schedule Training

In conjunction with crate training, schedule training is most effective. Schedule training works because puppy elimination is pretty predictable, and if you always take your puppy to the correct "potty spot" when you know he needs to go, you automatically help him to succeed. Schedule training is a highly effective, if temporarily tiresome, method for teaching your Bulldog exactly where he is supposed to relieve himself, complete with ample positive reinforcement. All you need to know to succeed at schedule training is that puppies typically need to go "potty":

- First thing in the morning.
- If they wake up during the middle of the night.
- After a nap.
- After an active play session.
- Within about 15 minutes after eating a meal or drinking water.
- Last thing before bedtime.
- About once an hour during the day in the first 12 weeks.

Putting the Pieces Together

Now it's time to combine the two methods. Every day, with as much consistency as is humanly possible (the more consistent you are, the sooner you will be rewarded with a housetrained puppy, so that's *your* positive reinforcement!), begin the morning by taking your Bulldog puppy outside to the preferred spot. Go out with him; don't just put him out in the yard and take him out on his leash. Stand there with him, holding the leash, until he relieves himself. Don't let him wander around the yard, play with him, or do anything else fun until he does his duty.

Getting the right crate, such as the Nylabone® Fold-Away Pet Carrier, will make housetraining easier.

As soon as he does what you want him to do, preferably while he is doing it, say the word "potty" or whatever other word you want him to associate with this action. Then, when he is done, heap on the praise like you've never heaped on praise before. "Oh, what a *good, good, good* doggy!" "What a *smart* doggy!" "Very, very *good* job at going potty!" Take off the leash and let him romp and play. Toss him a toy. Pet him, kiss him, give him a treat, whatever will help your puppy to understand that pottying, right there, in that very spot, is one of the most rewarding things he can possibly do.

After this first successful venture into the yard, bring your Bully back inside for breakfast. After breakfast, take him outside again and repeat the process. Then, bring him back inside for playtime or a rest in the crate if you can't watch him. About every hour, for the first 12 weeks or so, take your Bully outside, on the leash, and watch him until he does his business—then praise him. Also, even if it doesn't coincide with your hourly outings, remember to take him out after meals, after naps, and after active play sessions.

When you are watching your Bully inside, look for signs that he is getting ready to go, even if you feel like he just went. These signs include sniffing the ground intently and circling, as if he's looking for a good spot to go. Sweep him up and take him outside.

Every time your Bully "accidentally" goes inside, your progress is set back just a little. Always clean these spots thoroughly and spray them with an enzyme cleaner to remove any residual odor, because the odor will signal to your Bully that this spot is an acceptable potty spot. If you miss the signs and catch your Bully starting to potty in the house, give him a sharp "No!" and quickly take him outside. If he finishes out there, praise him! If he has already finished, just stand out there with him in the potty spot for a few minutes and let him sniff, to remind him where he is *supposed* to go.

Finally, remember that if your Bully puppy does have an accident in the house, *it isn't his fault, it's yours*. You weren't watching, you missed a cue, or you forgot (happens to the best of us!). But don't blame your Bully. Your sharp "No!" is your message to him that you don't like what he is doing, in contrast to the praise and kudos he gets for going in the correct place. Never ever swat your Bully or rub his nose in his accident! If you have to rub somebody's nose in it, it should be your own!

As your Bully gets older, he will have more bowel and bladder control and you won't need to take him out as often. After each meal, play session, and nap should be fine, as well as first thing in the morning and last thing at night. Eventually you won't have to go out there with him, either (unless you want to—he will enjoy the company). The point of going out with him and keeping him on his leash until he goes is simply to teach him what is expected. Once he knows and really understands, you won't need these tools anymore.

Patience is a virtue, as they say. Be patient in those early months, practice these steps consistently, and don't get lax with either the crate training or the schedule training until your puppy is at least six months old. Many pet owners quit being consistent about potty training too early, and puppies never fully learn. Give your Bully every chance at success. He really does want to be a good dog.

OBEDIENCE TRAINING AND SOCIALIZATION

The word "obedience" may not seem to apply very well to a Bulldog. Obedient? Well...maybe a more realistic term would be "good behavior training." Bulldogs have minds of their own and aren't particularly interested in following humans around and fawning on them. They would rather be the object of the fawning! (Who wouldn't?) Yet, Bulldogs are smart (even if they sometimes pretend not to hear a word you say) and perfectly capable of learning how to be well-behaved family members and human companions. All it takes is a little work.

Starting from puppyhood, you can do two very important things to help your Bulldog grow up into a happy, friendly, reliable companion: socialize and train.

Socialization

Socialization means exposing your Bulldog on a daily basis to different people, animals, and situations in a safe, positive setting. This teaches Bulldogs that the world is a friendly place and people and other dogs are not things to be feared. Socializing a Bulldog is not much different than socializing a person. We all need lots of positive contact with others to grow up confident, secure, and friendly.

Don't think that exposing your puppy to many different people will smother his natural guardian instinct. It won't. Bulldogs should have mellow, friendly temperaments, but any natural instinct to guard property or people, or to

Socialization with littermates when young will ensure that your Bulldog will get along with other dogs later in life.

"sense" when something is wrong or someone has bad intentions, will only become sharper and more refined by lots of experience with other humans and dogs. The more your Bulldog learns about people and dogs, the more he will understand which ones are trustworthy and which ones aren't. Socialization is life experience training for your Bulldog. It doesn't make him "soft." It makes him "smart." Just like people, some Bulldogs will naturally be friendly to all and others will be more reserved, but socialization is crucial for all dogs. (Besides, the look of a big, burly Bulldog in the window is enough to deter most evildoers.)

Training

Good behavior training is also important because it helps you to establish house rules and basic behaviors. Training the basic commands—sit, stay, come, down, heel—sets the stage for more advanced commands, whether in terms of competitive obedience or even turning on the light switches and fetching the newspaper. Training gives your Bulldog something to do. Every dog needs a purpose and can benefit from special "jobs." Learning new tricks, useful behaviors, or engaging in organized competition will make the most of your Bulldog's brain by keeping him active, engaged, and focused. Sure, you can spend plenty of time lounging on the couch, but a daily training session, practicing old tricks and working on new ones, will make that "down time" even more rewarding. You and your Bulldog will be developing a system of communication that will further cement your relationship into something really special.

BASIC COMMANDS

Begin training your Bulldog as soon as he is comfortable in your home and knows his name. There are two very important things to remember when training your Bulldog. First, train the dog without any potential distractions. Second, keep all lessons very short. Eliminating any distraction is important because it is essential that you have your puppy's full attention. This is not possible if there are other people, other dogs, butterflies, or birds to play with. Also, if you are training a puppy, always remember that puppies have very short attention spans. Even when the pup has become a young adult, the maximum time you should train him would be about 20 minutes. However, you can give the puppy more than one lesson a day, three being as many as are recommended, each well apart. If you train any longer, the puppy will most likely become bored, and you will have to end the session on a down note, which you should never do.

Before beginning a lesson, always play a little game so that your Bulldog is in an active state of mind and more receptive to training. Likewise, always end lessons with playtime for the dog, and always end training on a high note,

Training should be a fun experience for dog and owner alike. Never yell at your Bulldog for failing to follow instructions.

praising your dog. This will really build his confidence.

The Come Command

The come command is possibly the most important command you can teach your dog, and it is important to teach him this command as a puppy—it may even save your dog's life someday. Knowing that your dog will come to you immediately when you call him will ensure that you can trust him to return to you if there is any kind of danger nearby. Teaching your dog to come when called should always be a pleasant experience. You should never call your Bulldog in order to scold or yell at him, or he will soon learn not to respond. When the dog comes to you, make sure to give him a lot of praise, petting, and, in the beginning, a treat. If he expects happy things when he reaches your side, you'll never have trouble getting your dog to come to you.

Start with your dog on a long lead about 20 feet in length. Have plenty of treats that your Bulldog likes. Walk the distance of the lead, and then crouch down and say, "Come." Make sure that you use a happy, excited tone of voice when you call the dog's name. Your Bulldog should come to you enthusiastically. If not, use the long lead to pull him toward you, continuing to use the happy tone of voice. Give him lots of praise and a treat when he gets there. Continue to use the long lead until your dog is consistently obeying your command.

The Sit Command

As with most basic commands, your Bulldog will learn the sit command in just a few lessons. One 15-minute les-

Your Bulldog should be trained to sit on command. The sit command is one of the easiest commands for your dog to learn.

son each day should do the trick in no time. Some trainers will advise you that you should not proceed to other commands until the previous one has been learned really well. However, a bright, young Bulldog is quite capable of handling more than one command per lesson and certainly per day. As time progresses, you will be going through each command as a matter of routine before attempting a new one. This is so the dog always starts, as well as ends, a lesson on a high note, having successfully completed something.

When teaching the sit command, first, get a treat that your dog really likes and hold it right by his nose, so that all his attention is focused on it. Raise the treat above his head and say, "Sit." Usually, the dog will follow the treat and automatically sit. If not, guide him into position. Give him the treat for being such a good dog and don't forget to praise him. After a while, your Bulldog will begin to associate the word "sit" with the action. Most dogs will catch on very quickly. Once your dog is sitting reliably with the treat, take it away and just use praise as a reward. Most dogs will tend to stand up at first, so immediately repeat the exercise. When your Bulldog understands the command and does it right away, you can slowly move backward so that you are a few feet away. If he attempts to come to you, simply place the dog back in the original position and start again. Do not attempt to keep the dog in the sit position for too long. Even a few seconds is a long time for a impatient, energetic puppy, and you do not want him to get bored with lessons before he has even begun them.

The Stay Command

The stay command should follow your sit lesson, but it can be very hard for puppies to understand. Remember that a puppy wants nothing more than to be at your side, so it will be hard for him to stay in one place while you walk away. You should only expect your dog to perform this command for a few seconds at first, and then gradually work up to longer periods of time.

Face your dog and say, "Sit." Now step backward, saying, "Stay." It is also very helpful to use the hand signal for stay—place your hand straight out, palm toward the dog's nose. Let the dog remain in the position for only a few seconds before coming back to him, giving lots of praise and a treat. Once your dog gets the hang of it, repeat the command again, but step farther back. If your dog gets up and comes to you, simply go back to the original position and start again. As your dog starts to understand the command, you can move farther and farther back.

Once your Bulldog is staying reliably from a short distance, the next test is to walk away after placing the dog. This will mean your back is to the dog, which will tempt him to follow you. Keep an eye over your shoulder, and the minute the dog starts to move, spin around, say, "Stay," and start over from the original position.

As the weeks go by, you can increase the length of time the dog is in the stay position—but two to three minutes is quite long enough for a puppy. If your puppy drops into a down position and is clearly more comfortable, that's fine. In the beginning, staying put is good enough!

The Down Command

From a dog's viewpoint, the down command is one of the more difficult ones to accept. This position is submissive in a wild pack situation. A timid dog will roll over, which is a natural gesture of submission. A bolder dog will want to get up and might back off, not wanting to submit to this command. The dog will feel that he is about to be punished, which would be the position in a natural environment. Once he comes to understand this is not the case and that there are rewards for obeying, your Bulldog will accept this position without any problem.

You may notice that some dogs will sit very quickly, but will respond to the down command more slowly. This is their way of saying that they will obey the command, but under protest!

There are two ways to teach this command. If your dog is more willing to please, the first method should work. Obviously, with a puppy, it will be easier to teach Down if you are kneeling next to him. First, have your dog sit and hold a treat in front of his nose. When his full attention is on the treat, start to lower the treat slowly to the ground, saying "Down." The dog should follow the treat with his head. Bring it out slowly in front of him. If you are really lucky, your Bulldog will slide his legs forward and lie down by himself. Give him the treat and lots of praise for being such a good dog.

For a dog that won't lie down on his own (and most puppies won't), you can try this method: After the puppy is sitting and focused on the treat, take the front legs and gently sweep them forward, at the same time saying, "Down." Release the legs and quickly apply light pressure on the shoulders with your left hand. Then quickly tell the dog how good he is, give the treat, and make a lot of fuss. Repeat two or three times only in one training session. The dog will learn over a few lessons. Remember that this is a very submissive act on the dog's behalf, so there is no need to rush matters.

The Heel Command

All dogs should be able to walk nicely on a leash without a tug-of-war with their owners. Teaching your Bulldog the heel command should follow leash training. Heeling is best done in a place where you have a wall or a fence to one side of you, because it will restrict the dog's movements so that you only have to contend with forward and backward situations. Again, it is better to do the lesson in private and not in a place where there will be many distractions.

There will be no need to use a slip collar on your dog, as you can be just as effective with a flat, buckle one. The leash should be approximately 6 feet long. You can adjust the space between you, your Bulldog, and the wall so that your pet has only a small amount of room to move sideways. It is also very helpful to have a treat in your hand so that your dog will be focused on you and stay by your side.

Hold the leash in your right hand and pass it through your left. As the dog moves ahead and pulls on the leash, stop walking, and say, "Heel." Lure the dog back to your side with the treat. When the dog is in this position, praise him and begin walking again. Repeat the whole exercise. Once the dog begins to get the message, you can use your left hand (with the treat inside of it) to pat the side of your knee so that your Bulldog is encouraged to keep close to your side.

When your dog understands the basics, you can mix up the lesson a little to keep him focused. Do an about-turn, or make a quick left or right. This will result in a sudden jerk as you move in the opposite direction. The dog will now be behind you, so you can pat your knee and say, "Heel." As soon as the pup is in the correct position, give him lots of praise. The puppy will now begin to associate certain words with certain actions.

Once the lesson is learned and the dog is heeling reliably, then you can change your pace from a slow walk to a quick one, and your Bulldog will adjust. The slow walk is always more difficult for most puppies, as they are usually anxious to be on the move. End the lesson when the dog is walking nicely beside you. Begin the lesson with a few sit commands so you're starting with success and praise.

Recall to Heel Command

When your dog is coming to the heel position from an off-leash situation—for instance, if he has been running free—he should do this in the correct manner. He should pass behind you and take up his position, then sit. To teach this command, have your Bulldog in front of you in the sit position with his collar and leash on. Hold the leash in your right hand. Give him the command to heel and pat your left knee. As the dog starts to move forward, use your right hand to guide him behind you. If you need to, you can hold the collar and walk the dog around the back of you to the desired position. You will need to repeat this a few times until the dog understands what you want.

When you have done this a number of times, you can try it without the collar and leash. If the dog comes up toward your left side, then bring him to the sit position in front of you. Hold his collar and walk the pup around the back of you. Your dog will eventually understand and automatically pass around your back each time. If the dog is already behind you when you recall him, then he should automatically come to your left side. If necessary, pat your left leg.

The No Command

Your Bulldog must obey the "no" command every time. Your Bulldog must understand it 100 percent. Most delinquent dogs—the jumpers, the barkers, and the biters—never learned this command. If your dog were to approach any potential danger, the no command, coupled with the come command, could save his life. You do not need a specific lesson for this command; it will most likely be used every day. You must be consistent and apply it every time your dog is doing something wrong. It is best, however, to be able to replace the negative command with something positive. This way, your dog will respond more quickly. For example, if your puppy is chewing on your shoe, tell him, "No!" and replace the shoe with a Nylabone®. Then give him lots of praise.

GOING TO SCHOOL

Puppy Kindergarten

Every Bulldog puppy should attend puppy kindergarten or any type of puppy class designed primarily around teaching very simple commands and encouraging socialization. These classes expose Bulldogs to lots of other dogs and lots of other people in a positive, fun environment. Choose a class with an instructor who advocates positive rather than punitive training methods. Puppies exposed to lots of happy and fun early experiences with other dogs and people are much more likely to grow up into well-behaved, friendly,

Although these Bulldog puppies are cute and innocent, without proper early training, they can grow up to be willful and disobedient. If you don't have the time to properly train your dog, consider taking him to a professional who can train him for you.

outgoing adult dogs.

Basic Training Classes

After your Bulldog graduates from puppy kindergarten, enroll him in a basic obedience class. Obedience class is no substitute for daily training practice, but it is an invaluable tool in making the most of that daily practice. A good obedience instructor will help you and your dog learn the basics and can also troubleshoot when something isn't working and you aren't sure why. A good obedience instructor will also be flexible, helping you to find a method—such as clicker training, lure-and-reward training, or other methods—that works for you and your Bulldog. Avoid trainers who advocate any kind of rough treatment or punishment.

Rough treatment for a Bulldog doesn't include the slip collar or "choke chain," however. While these types of collars can injure some dogs, they are actually effective in training Bulldogs, when used correctly. Their thick, sturdy necks won't be injured and the quick jerk and release of the slip collar is a signal to your Bulldog to adjust something or pay attention and get back to walking at your side. However, never yank or drag your Bulldog around with a slip collar. Use it properly and it can serve as an excellent training tool. Your obedience instructor can show you how to use one correctly.

Basic obedience will instruct you how to teach your Bulldog those core moves. "Sit" and "down" are the beginning steps for many more advanced tricks, but these lessons are also useful to calm an excited Bulldog and get him under control, whether he is jumping up on people or getting himself overheated. "Stay" and "come" are useful, not only for training sessions and as the basis of other moves, but also for your Bulldog's safety should he ever get out of your control, running towards traffic or other dangers. "Heel" makes walking your Bulldog much more pleasant. Who wants to be dragged down the street? That's no fun.

Canine Good Citizen®

Finally, if you and your Bulldog get really good at basic obedience commands, consider helping your dog earn his Canine Good Citizen® certificate. This program rewards well-behaved dogs that can pass a series of basic good-manners tests. Many local clubs offer classes specifically designed to help with these tests and then periodically sponsor the actual tests. You and your Bulldog can take the test as many times as you like until you pass, but not multiple times during one testing event. For more information on the Canine Good Citizen® certificate or for more information on competitive obedience, agility, conformation dog shows, and other dog events, as well as lots of interesting purebred dog information, visit the American Kennel Club website at www.akc.org.

Your Healthy Bulldog

Every purebred dog has particular health issues associated with his breed, and the Bulldog is no exception. While a well-bred Bulldog has every chance of living a long, healthy life, knowing the Bulldog's particular vulnerabilities can help you to best care for health problems that occur and may prevent future health problems. While Bulldogs are prone to certain health issues, that doesn't mean your Bulldog will develop them. However, knowing what to look for can make all the difference between spotting a problem early and treating it promptly, and missing something that could potentially threaten your Bulldog's health and well-being.

Your most important ally in keeping your Bulldog healthy is, of course, your veterinarian. Not every vet understands or appreciates this special breed, so shop around until you find a vet who has a good rapport with your Bulldog and experience in treating this breed. Vets should understand certain breed-specific issues, such as the Bulldog's

The Bulldog's flat face puts him at risk for certain health issues. Because of the shortened muzzle, he may have trouble breathing.

sensitivity to anesthesia and other medications. Once you've found a vet you and your Bulldog like and who has experience with the breed, follow his or her advice on vaccination schedules and other issues of health maintenance, such as heartworm and flea prevention, healthy skin maintenance, and dental care.

THE BULLDOG'S FLAT FACE

The Bulldog's unique facial structure immediately puts him at risk for a few basic problems. Like all brachycephalic (flat-faced) breeds, Bulldogs can be prone to respiratory problems. Their nasal passages are shorter than in breeds with longer muzzles, making the Bulldog particularly susceptible to overheating because warm air has less time to cool off when inhaled through such a short muzzle. The Bulldog's elongated soft palate can also cause breathing issues, and most Bulldogs snort, snuffle, and snore. These noises are a natural by-product of the flat face and aren't problems in themselves unless they worsen, in which case they could signal respiratory distress. Keep an ear out for changes in your Bulldog's regular breathing sounds.

Respiratory distress, along with fatigue, can also be a sign of heart failure, another reason to check with your vet if your Bulldog experiences a sudden breathing or behavioral change.

KEEP 'EM COOL!

Truly one of the most dangerous health issues for Bulldogs is overheating, because it can happen so quickly and easily. While Bulldogs need exercise, they should not run around for too long in hot weather. Just because a Bulldog

Taking your Bulldog outside for exercise is important, but you need to make sure he doesn't overdo it. Overheating can be extremely dangerous to a Bulldog.

This little Bulldog loves to play in tall grass. Check his coat thoroughly for ticks and other parasites upon returning inside. Contact your veterinarian about any questionable marks.

is having fun in the sun doesn't mean he will know when he's had enough. That's your job! Keep your Bulldog inside during hot weather, or take him out with you for short periods of time. Let him play in a child's plastic swimming pool, but never fill it deeper than the height of your Bulldog's chin. Their heavy heads keep Bulldogs from being good swimmers, so they shouldn't swim in deep water. They can drown easily.

During the summer, let your Bulldog chew on ice. Keep a big bowl of ice chips handy in the yard while outside. Inside, make sure he has access to cool air. Put his bed near an air conditioning vent, and always keep a bowl of ice accessible for chewing and play. Never leave your Bulldog alone outside on a hot day. You might forget he is out there, and you will miss any clues that he is becoming overheated. Your Bulldog might not think to come in until he is already suffering from heatstroke. Besides, many Bulldogs left alone in people's yards are stolen. The risk isn't worth it. Bring your Bully back inside with you when you've had enough summer fun.

Also, never leave a Bulldog alone in a car, no matter the weather! Not only is a Bulldog alone in a car an easy target for thieves, but the temperature inside a car can rise surprisingly quickly, even on a temperate day, and a Bulldog won't last long in a hot car. Keep walks brief and let your Bulldog get a lot of his exercise by playing with you inside. Bulldog owners must always keep temperature concerns in mind for their Bulldog's safety.

SENSITIVE SKIN ISSUES

The Bulldog's sensitive skin can easily

develop rashes, infections, fungus, eczema, acne around the muzzle and mouth, and hot spots. Hot spots are inflamed, weeping wound-like spots that itch and are difficult to heal and can be caused by a reaction to any number of environmental causes, such as fleas or reactions to certain food. Environmental factors may trigger many different skin problems in Bulldogs, depending on the dog, the dog's health, and probably genetic predispositions to certain problems.

Bulldogs also have a tendency to aggravate their irritated skin with constant licking and scratching, making the problem much worse and often causing infection. Watch your Bulldog for signs that he is scratching, licking, and rubbing a particular spot so you can treat the problem before it gets out of control. A skin infection can be very difficult to resolve.

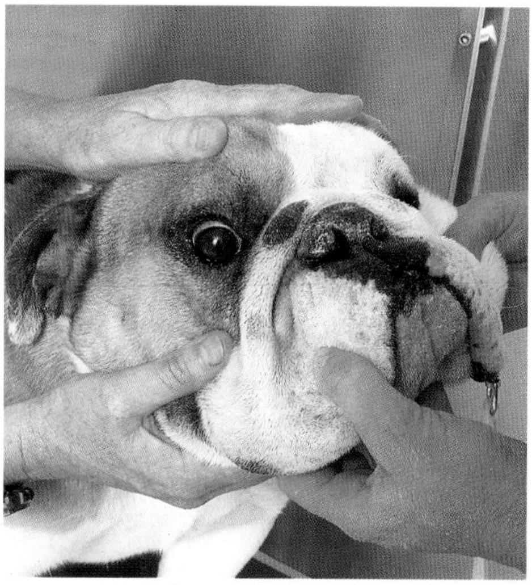

Your Bulldog's eyes should always be dark, clear, and free from any redness or irritation.

To keep your Bulldog's skin in good health, remember the daily rubdown mentioned in the last section on grooming. This will help keep up the necessary protective oil production in your Bulldog's skin. A high-quality food can also make a big difference in skin health, as can preventive pest control. If your Bulldog never gets a fleabite, his skin won't ever have the chance to develop fleabite dermatitis!

Bulldogs can also develop interdigital cysts, which are big red bumps between the Bulldog's toes. Ask your veterinarian what to use to relieve these cysts. Another common skin problem in Bulldogs is bacterial infections within his skin folds. Keeping skin folds immaculately clean and dry will help to prevent this problem, but if an infection develops, see your vet for treatment. Some Bulldogs have a partially or fully receded tail, and this skin pocket must also stay clean and dry. The Bulldog may also experience infection of the hair follicles or other various lumps and bumps. Again, that daily rubdown will help you to catch any skin changes early. Let your vet take a look at anything suspicious.

EYE ISSUES

Bulldogs also have sensitive eyes, which can easily become dry and irritated by wind, dust, and other airborne particles like smoke and pollen. For Bulldogs that tend to have dry eyes, a daily dose of vet-recommended moisturizing eye drops can relieve this problem and prevent more serious problems like cornea damage or cherry eye.

More serious eye issues include cherry eye, in which the gland under the lower eyelid pops out and requires treatment from a vet, and genetic conditions like ectropion or entropion, where the eyelid rolls outward or inward (respectively) and the eyelashes can scratch the cornea, causing corneal abrasions or ulcers. Any clouding of the cornea could indicate cataracts. If you notice any changes in your Bulldog's eyes or their surrounding area, see your veterinarian.

BULLDOG ORTHOPEDICS

The Bulldog's heavy head, broad shoulders, and narrow hips should be balanced, stable, and sound, but some Bulldogs do experience occasional orthopedic issues. Bulldogs can be prone to hip dysplasia, as well as shoulder and elbow problems. Keep an eye out for changes in movement or joints that suddenly seem painful or swollen. Like any dog, Bulldogs may also develop osteoarthritis as they age.

A healthy diet and, if your vet recommends it, supplementation with a joint formula made for pets containing glucosamine and chondroitin sulfate, may help to strengthen the elbow joint and prevent or lessen the effects of osteoarthritis. Also, a Bulldog that gets plenty of exercise on a regular basis and doesn't become overweight will have strong muscles that will help to keep elbow joints firmly in place. In addition, a well-exercised Bulldog won't stress his joints as much as an overweight dog might. These are just a few more reasons not to let your Bulldog become a couch potato!

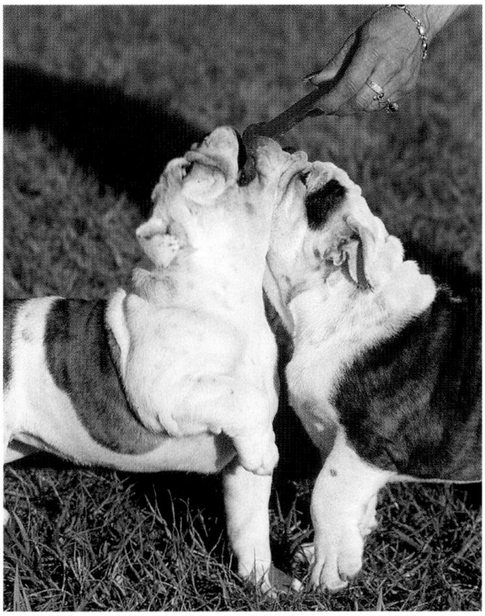

Safe chew toys, such as those made by Nylabone®, are essential. Toys that can splinter or break are choking hazards.

DENTAL ISSUES

The Bulldog has a large but foreshortened face, and sometimes Bulldogs will develop dental malformations—crowded, missing, or deformed teeth, or jaw problems. Keep your Bulldog's teeth clean, and if he has trouble eating his food or seems to be in pain, see your vet.

While destructive chewing may not be exactly a dental issue, it is certainly a Bulldog issue. Bulldogs have strong mouths and many chew enthusiastically, well past puppyhood when other breeds have lost interest in gutting couch cushions or gnawing off all the baseboards. Bulldogs need outlets for all that chewing energy and should have plenty of sturdy chew toys, such as those made by Nylabone®. Chewing is a health issue because Bulldogs can easily chew off small pieces of hard objects that then become a choking hazard. They can also chew and eat garbage and other potentially toxic substances.

Bulldog-proof your house by keeping dangerous items out of reach and by strictly enforcing the chew-toy-only rule. Whenever your Bulldog starts to chew something other than his chew toy, a sharp "No!" and a quick bait-and-switch (remove Bulldog from wrong object, immediately deliver chew toy) followed by praise for chewing the toy will quickly teach your Bulldog what he may and may not chew. This will not only preserve your furniture, shoes, and house but is much safer for your Bulldog.

BULLDOG BREEDING ISSUES

Bulldog breeding is not for the faint-hearted. The female Bulldog's small pelvis make whelping difficult, and most females must have Cesarean sections to give birth to their litters. Because they are particularly sensitive to anesthesia, this surgery puts the mother at risk. Bulldog breeding is a hobby that should be reserved only for those willing to take the risk, experience the occasional tragic loss, and pay the astronomical vet bill. Breeding Bulldogs is not profitable, and good hobby breeders only do it because they are so devoted to the breed that they want to work to preserve and improve Bulldogs. Anyone else, no matter how much they love their pets, should have their Bulldogs spayed or neutered.

TRAINING AND GOOD HEALTH

Why is a well-trained Bulldog a healthier Bulldog? Because Bulldogs that behave and follow the rules, that have developed bonded relationships with their people, and that understand basic commands are less likely to fall prey to many different health and life-threatening scenarios, such as wandering and being hit by a car, getting involved in dog fights, biting a person, or being relinquished to an animal shelter for being impossible to live with.

Train, socialize, love, and care for your Bulldog. Give him high-quality food, groom him well, keep him clean, and give him all the cuddles and kisses you can spare. You'll be rewarded with a healthy, happy, well-mannered, burly little buddy that will give you years of love, companionship, and affection in return.

Resources

Bulldog Club of America
Corresponding Secretary: Kathy Moss
22031 Britt Oaks Drive
Norman, TX 77511
www.thebca.org

American Kennel Club
Headquarters:
260 Madison Avenue
New York, NY 10016

Operations Center:
5580 Centerview Drive
Raleigh, NC 27606-3390

Customer Services:
Phone: (919) 233-9767
Fax: (919) 816-3627
www.akc.org

The Kennel Club
1 Clarges Street
London
W1J 8AB
Phone: 087 0606 6750
Fax: 020 7518 1058
www.the-kennel-club.org.uk

The Canadian Kennel Club
89 Skyway Avenue
Suite 100
Etobicoke, Ontario, Canada
M9W 6R4
Order Desk & Membership: 1-800-250-8040
Fax: (416) 675-6506
www.ckc.ca

The United Kennel Club, Inc.
100 E. Kilgore Road
Kalamazoo, MI 49002-5584
(616) 343-9020
www.ukcdogs.com

Index

Photo Credits

All photos by Isabelle Francais